THE HORSE HEAD FROM WALDGIRMES

A PARTICULAR STROKE OF LUCK

The final year of excavations conducted in Wald-girmes by the Romano-Germanic Commission of the German Archaeological Institute was to have been 2009. In previous years, large parts of the Roman city had already been explored and archaeologically investigated.

In the final excavation campaign, only a Roman well inside the settlement behind the western gate of the defensive wall remained to be examined.

In the autumn of 2008, scientific investigations took place in preparation for the upcoming excavation. A core was drilled to determine the well's depth. By using computer tomography, scientists from the University of Heidelberg were able to confirm a developed depth of at least 6 m. The archaeologists felt well informed at the start of the excavation and expected no surprises.

Therefore, they were all the more astonished when the head of a horse made of bronze was discovered in a wooden barrel at the bottom of the well shaft – buried under millstones. At first glance, the excavators recognised in the muddy find the extraordinary quality of the sculptor's work, which was confirmed after the initial cleaning.

Although various equine sculptures from the ancient world are presently known, only a few reach a comparable level of artistry. Of particular importance for its historical classification is the statue's find spot and with it the precise dating to the period between 4 BC and AD 16. This precision makes the find a particular stroke of luck for the field of art history. Thanks to this last-minute discovery, the many bronze fragments found earlier, and indeed the entire excavation in Waldgirmes could be viewed in a new light. The possible reconstruction of the forum complex with equestrian statues made of gilded bronze gave the urban setting a new historical dimension. CA

-2 m
-3 m
-4 m
-5 m
-6 m
-7 m
-8 m
-9 m
-10 m
-11 m

THE HORSE IN THE WELL

In 2009, the bronze horse head was recovered from a well on the settlement's east-west-running road. The technically demanding excavation exposed the well shaft to a depth of 11 m. Beyond a certain depth, due to safety considerations, the work had to be carried out as in an open-pit mine. By using heavy equipment, the pit was secured with sloping walls and a vehicle access ramp.

During the excavation, the well shaft was cut in half so the soil could be removed layer by layer. After each layer was removed, the excavators cleaned the resulting profile and documented it with a photograph. These photographs were later assembled on three-dimensionally-measured points to create a complete picture. Thus, it is possible to present a true-to-original cross-section of the entire well shaft, from top to bottom.

At the bottom of the shaft, a discarded barrel formed the well chamber. The horse head was found just above the bottom of the well, wedged in among eight millstones. The head lay on an almost unused millstone and was covered by another. The right foot of the equestrian statue was on the rim of the barrel.

The position of the finds shows that the millstones and statuary fragments were thrown into the well at the same time.

Above this, the well's timber lining was preserved to a height of four metres. This additional structure was made from split oak planks. The outer and inner surfaces of the planks were sealed with a coating of clay, so that water could only rise into the well from below.

Dendrochronological dating of the well's timber dates its construction to 4 BC. A coin with a counterstamp of Varus, found in the middle of the shaft, as well as the many contemporaneous potsherds, suggest that the well was wholly and deliberately backfilled after the year AD 7.   CA

FROM WAX TO BRONZE — THE PRODUCTION PROCESS

Casting seam on the inner side of a statue fragment.

Bronzesmiths cast the statues in separate parts, using the so-called indirect method of lost-wax casting. Clear traces of the production process can still be seen on many of the fragments.

In a first step, the sculptor created a full-size model in clay; he then encased its various parts with plaster. These negative plaster moulds were placed next to one another, and their inside surfaces coated with wax. For this, warmed wax sheets could be used, which would easily stick to the plaster. Alternatively, liquid wax might be poured on or applied with a brush, creating positive partial forms in wax. Larger hollow elements like the horse's head will have been filled with an additional clay casting core for stability. The plaster moulds with the wax layer inside were covered with clay, creating a closed casting mould. Next, the mould was heated to fire the clay and melt the wax, which flowed out through hollow channels (sprues). The bronzesmith then filled the cavity with molten bronze. After cooling the mould, he broke it open, thus obtaining a bronze figure in the shape of the wax model. Large statues like this one were cast in multiple sections; these were later assembled and soldered together. Subsequent cold-working of the surface removed the sprues and retouched casting defects and seams. Details were engraved. Finally, the surface was gilded with thin gold leaf.

The complex bronze casting of the equestrian statues was apparently not done in Waldgirmes. Traces of a large workshop have not been found there. It remains unclear whether the statues were delivered in completed form or in parts that were assembled on site. During the assembly of the individual parts, it would have been possible for the craftsmen to address special wishes of their clients, such as by decorating the harness with different medallions. It is also unclear where the casting was carried out. The skilled know-how was undoubtedly available in nearby Gaul or the larger settlements along the Rhine. **CA**

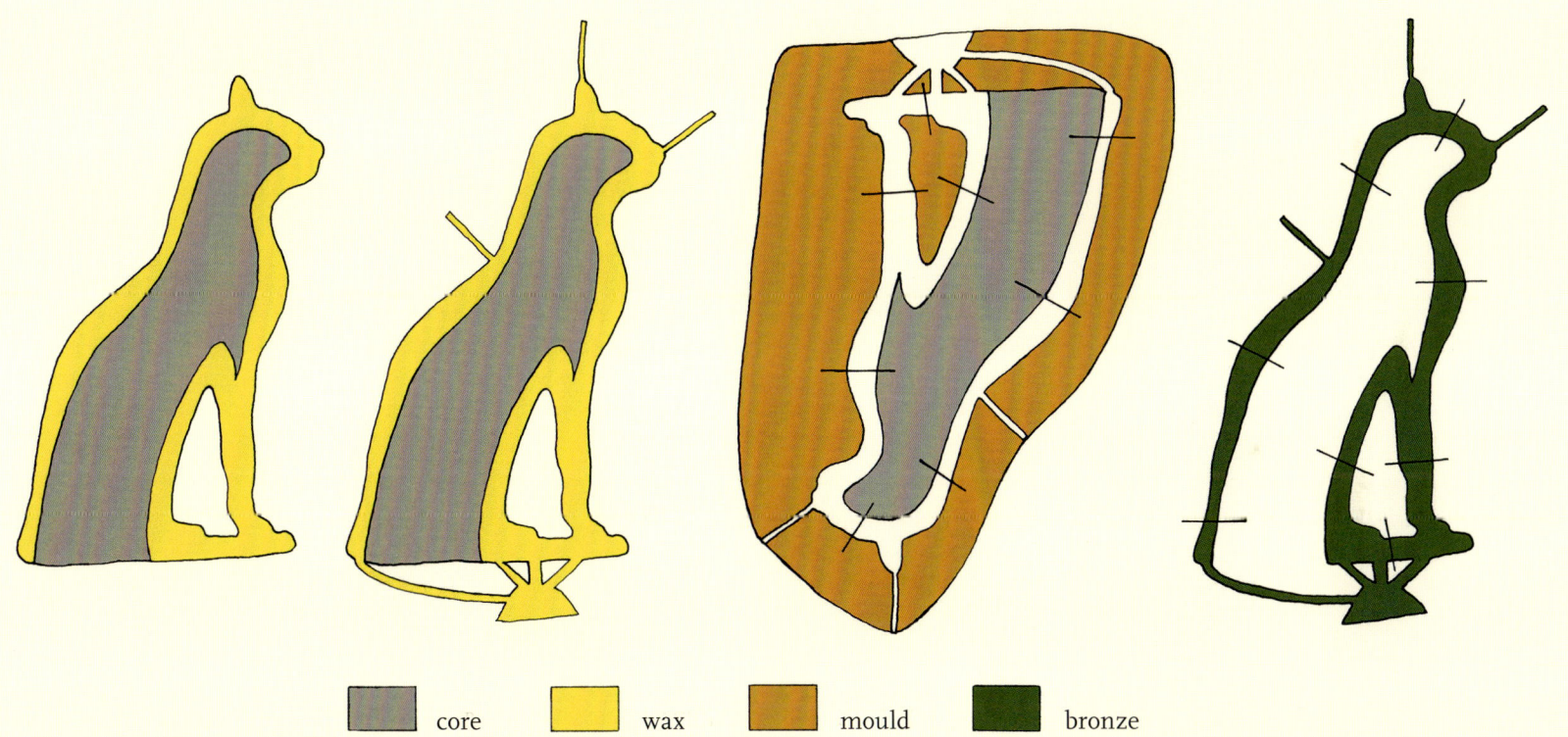

core   wax   mould   bronze

THE PHOENIX FROM THE WELL

Restoration of the gilded bronze fragments and the horse's head took place in the workshops of hessenARCHÄOLOGIE in the State Office for the Preservation of Historical Monuments.

The horse head made of gilded bronze had spent about 2,000 years at the bottom of the Roman well at a depth of approximately 11 metres in a wet environment where no oxygen could reach it. Therefore its state of preservation was relatively good. However, corrosion products of bronze were deposited at many places on the sculpture's gold surface and had become firmly attached to it. Freeing the horse head from these deposits proved to be very challenging, because of the great brittleness of the gold leaf coating.

For this reason, conservator Angelika Ulbrich paid particular attention to removing the corrosion without endangering the gold surface. She worked exclusively with a microscope, using polishing elements made of silicone. In some places she had to reinforce the surface with acrylic resin; finally, the entire surface was sealed with a thin protective coating of acrylic resin.

During the process, further questions arose. In particular, the techniques used to produce such a bronze statue needed to be understood in detail. The gold content of the gold leaf and the methods used in its application also required clarification. Last but not least, metal analyses were needed to clarify the composition of the bronze alloy, in order to possibly provide information about the place where the statue had been made.

A careful examination of the traces of construction on the inner surfaces of the horse's head made it possible to reconstruct the entire manufacturing process. Marks left during the lost wax technique, such as imprints of overlapping wax sheets, wax drops, brushstrokes, or even the fingerprints of the craftsmen, bring to life every step of the elaborate procedure and testify to the exceptional craftsmanship of Roman bronzesmiths. CA

The horse head before restoration.

"THE HORSE UPLIFTS HIS HEAD EAGERLY AS IF TO BREAK INTO FULL CAREER"

(STATIUS, SILVAE)

A life-size, 59 cm long, gilded horse head from an equestrian statue is the most prominent find from Waldgirmes. At first glance, the viewer is captivated by the great liveliness and plasticity with which the sculptor has captured the structure and appearance of the head. The reproduction of the individual details of the muscles, nostrils and eyes testifies to superior craftsmanship and artistic perceptiveness.

Various medallions at the intersections of the straps and on the noseband decorate the bridle. Of the original four lateral decorative discs, one is missing. The other three discs display in low relief busts of the goddess of victory, Victoria, identified by the wings on her back. A round medallion with a bust whose head has been lost adorns the browband. Additional decorative elements were mortised in the holes to the right and left of the disc. In the centre of the horse's face is a larger oval medallion showing the god of war, Mars, sitting naked on a rock, with a cloak thrown over his left shoulder. On his head, he wears a helmet with a high crest. His left arm rests on a standing shield, while he grips a sword in his right hand. The alignment of the decorative discs shows that the horse's

head originally was drawn downwards by tightened reins. The equestrian statue of Marcus Aurelius on the Capitol in Rome provides an approximate idea of the position of horse and rider.

While the design of the Waldgirmes horse head and its bridle show great skill, the depictions in the medallions are comparatively clumsy. It is therefore probable that the head itself was made in one of the centres of bronze casting. The best comparisons to the find from Waldgirmes are the horse heads from Pergola di Cartoceto in northern Italy, which for stylistic reasons date to the period between 50 and 30 BC.

For the dating of the head from Waldgirmes, the precise data for the settlement's existence provide clear evidence.
                                                                    CA

THE EMPEROR AT THE FORUM

The layout of the Forum in Waldgirmes belongs to a later expansion phase of the settlement. Its architectural design with the columned halls on three sides and the transverse basilica is seen in many similar Augustan-era complexes in Gaul, Italy and Spain. These were monumental edifices whose models may be found in the imperial architecture of Rome. The arrangement of the five statue pedestals in front of the Basilica in the Forum's courtyard corresponds to the axisymmetric placement of statues typical of such places.

There is no concrete evidence identifying the depicted persons. Based on comparable statuary programs and the Forum of Augustus in Rome, dedicated in 2 BC, we can reckon with a representation of Augustus and members of his imperial household. In the centre may have stood an equestrian statue of Augustus wearing armour, flanked by militarily accomplished relatives like Drusus Major, Germanicus or Tiberius, and the sons of Agrippa, Gaius and Lucius. Such a group of horsemen would have publicly displayed Augustus' claim to power and succession plan. The military virtues of the depicted persons are also reflected in the decorative medallions on the harness of the only pre-

served horse's head. The combination of the images of Mars and Victoria points up the martial aspect.

The evocative arrangement of the dynastic statuary group of Augustus and his male relatives on the Forum marks the ideational centre of the newly founded settlement of Waldgirmes. Cities usually donated such commemorative statues as a sign of their loyalty to the reigning emperor and in recognition of the Roman system of rule.

The statues probably stood for only a few years between AD 7 and 9. According to dendrochronological data, their destruction – combined with a fire that devastated the surrounding buildings – occurred at the end of the year 9 or early in 10 AD. This timing suggests a connection between the destruction of the entire complex and the catastrophic defeat of the Romans in the Varian Disaster of AD 9. CA

THE PUZZLE

During the excavations in Waldgirmes, a total of 160 fragments of gilded bronze were found, with a total weight of about 22 kg. These would make up only a small portion of a complete bronze statue. The fragments were scattered all over the site, but the majority came from the roadside ditches along the main street, the Forum, the well and a hoard found just outside the western gate. Only four of the fragments fit together.

The left foot of a rider, clad in a senator's boot (calceus), comes from the well in which the horse head was discovered. This fragment shows no traces of gilding, and therefore it is doubtful that the horse's head and the shoe belonged to the same statue. The smaller gilded fragments with curls of hair could come from the head of a rider. Remnants of the folds of a garment may be a rider's clothing. In addition to the horse's head, a horse's foot, as well as larger fragments of breast-harness with vegetal ornamentation, are preserved. A notable fragment is thought to be the penile sheath or foreskin of a horse.

The distribution of the statue fragments and the provenience of the finds permit us to hypothesise about the events that led to the destruction of the forum's statues. The statues were probably broken down on the spot, the better to melt them down for reuse of the metal. This explains the many splinters of bronze found in the Forum, above all around the site of the statues. The reuse of the bronze as a raw material for casting also explains the discovery of a gold-plated fragment in Wetzlar-Dalheim, 5 km distant.

The large fragments of the horse's head, foot, penile sheath and harness seem to have been deliberately deposited. Such depositions are known in antiquity from many different cultures. Wells, moors or other places with a relationship to water are often used to deposit statues or parts of statues. A consistent interpretation of these various depositions has yet to be found. CA

NOT FROM THE SAME HORSE

Among the gilded fragments of bronze are three pieces from the breast-strap of the harness. The most sizeable piece, weighing 3.5 kg, came to light in the ditch in front of the Forum; the two smaller ones lay in the defensive ditch in front of the west gate.

Although the three pieces do not fit together, they do show a similar decorative principle: the curling tendril of an acanthus plant fills a narrow area between flanking borders. From the expanding tendrils, two tiny leaves emerge at regular intervals. Alternating above and below the tendrils, small, four-petalled flowers appear between the leaflets.

Two lateral terminals have survived, whose corners are decorated with sculpted buttons. Remains of the harness breast band, which was usually figuratively decorated, are not among the fragments found.

A comparison shows that the fragments were not cast in the same mould and therefore probably were not associated with a single horse. The two smaller ones seem to have been cast together with the horse's body. The larger piece, on the other hand, could have been made separately and then attached to the statue of the horse. These dissimilarities in the manufacturing process and the different designs of the decorative acanthus tendril rule out the association of these three fragments with a single statue. CA

THE WALDGIRMES SETTLEMENT

Sites, Augustan-Tiberian period, military

Sites, Augustan-Tiberian period, civil

Sites, Augustan-Tiberian period, unproven

Site of the Varian Disaster

Winsum

Bentumersiel

Ems

Elbe

Velsen I

Kalkriese

Hannover-Wilkenburg

Porta Westfalica (Barkhausen)

Bunnik-Vechten

Arnheim-Meinerswijk

Nederrijn

Sparrenberger Egge

Bevern

IJssel

Nijmegen

Lek

Waal

Maas

Kalkar-Altkalkar

Haltern

Anreppen

Köln-Alteburg

Olfen

Oberaden

Xanten-Vetera I

Holsterhausen

Werl

Hedemünden

Kneblinghausen

Moers-Asberg

Kring

Neuss

Köln-Alteburg

Schelde (Stadt)

Asse

Bonn

Remagen

Waldgirmes

Lahnau-Dorlar

Arnsburg

Weser

Urmitz

Bad Nauheim

Rödgen

Andernach

Lahnstein-Schmidtenhöhe

Lahnstein-Becheln

Friedberg (Am steinernen Kreuz)

Karben-Okarben

Arras LaCorette

Frankfurt-Hoechst

Main

Hofheim Erdlager

Rhein

Wederath

Mainz

Trebur-Geinsheim

Bad Kreuznach

Alzey

Gernsheim

0   50   100 km

THE SITE IN THE "GOLDEN FIELD"

View of modern Waldgirmes; the Dünsberg rises in the background.

The RGK's excavations began in 1993 on the western edge of Lahnau-Waldgirmes with a trial trench excavated on a plot of land known as the "Goldener Acker" (Golden Field). Subsequent excavations and geophysical measurements initially showed a double trench system, which was interpreted as the trapezoidal defences of a military camp. Soon, however, traces of buildings and columned halls emerged along a broad street. The realisation that this was not a military camp but instead a civil settlement – and one that had only existed in the time of Augustus – led to a new research approach.

Since the beginnings of Limes research in Germany in the late 19th century, an important question has been the relationship between the Germanic peoples living beyond the borders of the empire and their new neighbours. Roman finds were known from Germanic territory stretching from so-called Free Germania to Scandinavia. Germanic settlement in the Limes' immediate vicinity, however, was only unequivocally proven with burial finds from the valley of the River Lahn. Therefore, the area around the towns of Gießen and Wetzlar became a major focus of the "Romanisation" project, funded by the German Research Foundation (DFG) from 1993 to 1999. During the project's preparatory phase, a volunteer at the State Office for the Preservation of Historical Monuments alerted archaeologists from the Frankfurt office of the Romano-Germanic Commission (RGK) to finds from Waldgirmes. There, in addition to Germanic pottery, Roman potsherds from the reign of Emperor Augustus had been discovered during several surveys.

From 1993 to 2009, the area was archaeologically investigated through a cooperative project involving the RGK, the Hesse State Department of Archaeology, the DFG, the community of Lahnau-Waldgirmes, the Lahn-Dill-District and a local booster club, founded in 1995. The aim was the large-scale examination of the complex's interior. As far as possible, the excavation areas created should record interrelated building structures. By the end of the project, 4.4 ha of the total 8 ha settlement could be excavated. CA

ARCHAEOLOGY WITHOUT SPADES

When investigating archaeological sites today, in addition to traditional methods such as surveys or aerial photography, geophysical methods are increasingly used. These are particularly promising when the characteristics of archaeological structures in the soil differ significantly from their environment. Since the 1960s, archaeological prospection has utilised various techniques of geoelectric mapping and measuring with ground-penetrating radar. However, the geomagnetic method is that most commonly and successfully employed. It measures the ways various materials in the soil, such as pit fillings or walls, influence the earth's magnetic field in contrast to the natural soil.

In Waldgirmes, geophysical surveys have been conducted since 1993 on a total of 23.3 hectares of arable land. Taking into account the predominantly small-scale ownership of property, readings were taken in a series of rectangles that were systematically walked. Finds of potsherds prompted an initial investigation of areas north of the modern town's boundaries. After adjusting the results to exclude the magnetic influence of a warehouse built with iron girders, clear traces of settlement were found: filled pits and above all the drainage ditch, which ran down the middle of the broad, east-west-running road.

In 1998, the Forum was excavated, and with it, the civilian character of the settlement revealed. The geophysical surveys were therefore relocated to focus on that area from 2000 to 2004. Thanks to the geophysical data, a marching camp for Roman troops could be identified in front of the east gate. Beneath the later Roman settlement, an Iron Age burial ground covering 12 ha was discovered. During geomagnetic surveys conducted in 2007 within the enclosure, using a much smaller grid, it was even possible to detect narrow foundation-, fence- and drainage ditches as well as individual postholes. This information made possible the reconstruction of the internal structure of various building complexes, which were then confirmed and supplemented by targeted excavations.

CA

THE INFRASTRUCTURE OF THE SETTLEMENT

A wall, more than three metres thick, surrounded the town. Its facade of wooden planks was backed by packed earth, reinforced by a timber box construction. In front of the wall, two V-shaped ditches, more than two metres deep and eight metres wide, provided additional protection. Gates on each of the four sides provided access to the town (the southern gate could not be excavated because of overbuilding). The total area had a trapezoidal layout and covered around 7.7 ha.

Two streets, running east-west and north-south, crossed the town and linked the city gates. The Forum was sited just north of the place where the two roads met. These streets divided the urban area and provided the orientation for the various building complexes. Excavations revealed ditches along both sides of the streets.

Two wells could be unearthed in the town. Dendrochronological analysis of their timber lining shows that they were dug in 4/3 BC. Thus, the wells provide a firm and accurate date for the start of construction work in the town. The wells also provide clear evidence for the end of Roman settlement after AD 9/10.

Well 2 in the western part of the city served as a public water source. The life-sized, gilded bronze horse head from one of the equestrian statues on the Forum was found in the shaft of this well. Clearly, two wells could not supply enough water for the needs of an entire town. The nearby Lahn River probably also served as a source of fresh water.

Two buildings in the western part of the settlement may be barracks that housed soldiers. Their floor plans are reminiscent of the barracks that were also built in Roman military bases during the same period. Soldiers not only assumed police duties but were also responsible for the construction and maintenance of essential infrastructure in Roman towns.

CA

The foundations of the Forum
in an aerial photo.

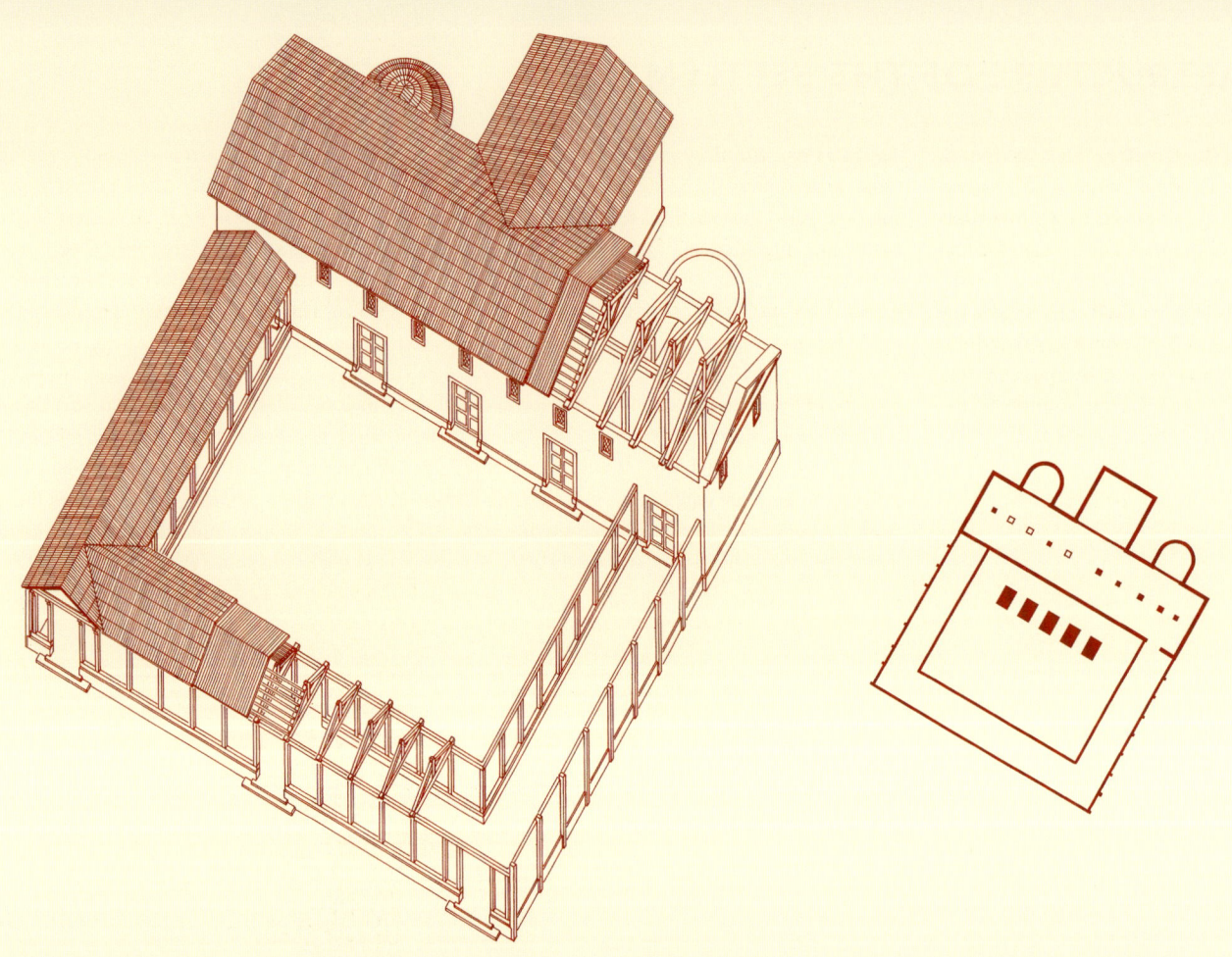

EVERYDAY LIFE IN WALDGIRMES

The Forum, covering an area of 44 x 43 metres, was in the centre of town. It was the only building complex that stood on stone foundations; its walls were constructed in half-timber work. From the Augustan period, no other structure with stone foundations is presently known east of the Rhine. Columned arcades (porticoes) stood on three sides of an interior courtyard, closed off by a great hall (basilica). In the courtyard, the remains of five rectangular pedestals were discovered. Numerous fragments of gilded bronze, also found in this area, will have come from equestrian statues on the pedestals.

Traces of wooden and half-timbered buildings show up as discolourations in the soil. Some of the houses were ambitious structures (see the excavation plan at the end of this Guide). From the doorway, one entered a roughly square space in the centre of the house. Above this interior room (atrium), there was an open skylight. The living areas and bedrooms were grouped around the atrium, receiving light through their doorways since the windows were small and placed high in the outer walls.

An additional group of buildings, with roofed arcades (porticoes) and rooms open to the street, appear to have been shops (tabernae). Here, artisans made and sold their products. Presumably, some of the buildings also had an upper storey in which living quarters and bedrooms were located. The artisans' houses mostly stood along the roads.

For the most part on the fringes of the settlement, there are numerous structures thought to be storehouses. In those identified so far, the building's floor was raised above ground level, supported by timber posts. Such construction offered protection against insects and vermin, and also ensured better ventilation for the stored supplies. Simple sheds or warehouses, partially open to the elements, were also found. CA

PRAESIDIUM, COLONIA OR COLONIA NOVA?

As soon as the first archaeological discoveries were made at Waldgirmes, there arose the question of whether this had been a military or a civilian complex. First of all, fortification systems with double ditches and timber walls backed with earth are very well known from military bases. Also, the T-shaped street plan strongly resembles that seen in such bases: an arrangement of two main streets that connect opposing gateways. As the excavation progressed, it became more and more probable that the planned installation of the infrastructure with roads, fortifications and water supply had indeed been carried out by the military. This interpretation is also supported by two buildings from the time of the town's founding, which are thought to be military barracks with a detached suite of rooms at one end of the barrack.

In contrast, construction within the walls follows civil settlement patterns. The streets are lined with houses fronted by porches under which are shops and workshops that open onto the road. The regular arrangement of buildings south of the main east-west-running street recalls the blocks built in Roman settlements. The representative Forum in the centre contributes very significantly to the urban character of the settlement. However, the dimensions and furnishings of the Forum complex seem oversized in relation to the assumed number of residents and the quality of the other buildings. It can, therefore, be assumed that the construction of the Forum between AD 5/6 and AD 9 was connected to an administrative change in the importance of the settlement and, with it, a demonstration of the Roman claim to power. The status of Waldgirmes before the start of construction is best described by the term "praesidium" (fortified military post). But the construction of the monumental Forum and the installation of the representative group of statues suggest that Waldgirmes was intended to develop into one of the Roman "coloniae novae" mentioned by Tacitus. The installation of Waldgirmes should thus be regarded as a building block in the establishment of a Roman province in Germania east of the Rhine. With the retreat of the Romans from Germania in AD 16, however, this plan could no longer be realised. CA

DISTRICTS AND UTILISATION

Within the settlement of Waldgirmes, varied types of buildings and areas of usage can be identified from excavated evidence. The Forum, with its impressive size and striking architecture, was at the centre of the complex and served representative purposes.

Several hall-like buildings with large interiors, as well as a storehouse supported on numerous posts, characterise construction in the area of the western defences. The material recovered here included not only slag, grindstones and millstones but also heavy pottery as well as scattered tools and military equipment. Apparently, this was an area used less for residential purposes than for warehousing, production and maintenance work. Here, too, stood the long structures, thought to be military barracks. The area south of the road was mostly undeveloped and delimited to the south by a fence or a palisade. All in all, this picture suggests a particular use of the sector on either side of the road, possibly by the town's central administration or the military.

Southeast of the intersection, a row of buildings with continuous porticoes extended along the main east-west road. The buildings were each divided into several smaller rooms and show traces of craft production in the form of tools, factory waste and associated facilities. This seems to have been a cluster of Roman artisan's houses, with living and sleeping areas in the rear part of each building and a workshop with sales-room facing the street, such as are known from other Roman settlements.

In the northeastern area, there was evidence for several spacious buildings of light construction. They were partially open to the elements, and their floor plans were either undivided or only slightly divided. These are likely to have been covered workshops and sheds, suitable for a variety of production and craft activities. RS

VARIED TRADES

The documented buildings were all erected in half-timber construction, which points to the vital role of carpentry. Carefully trimmed beams were predominantly used, as shown by the supporting posts, which regularly display a rectangular cross-section. Because there is no evidence of slate shingles or clay roof tiles, it is likely that the buildings were roofed with organic materials. The use of wood shingles would be an obvious choice; a splitting knife from the find material could have been used in this context.

For the work of construction, forged products of various kinds were needed, such as structural iron, fittings, clamps and nails as well as locks. Occasionally, these items appear among the finds, but blacksmithing is mainly proved by a workstation in one of the artisan's houses and by several pits containing slag and iron scale, which are waste products in iron production and forging. A partially-completed, solid-hilted iron knife from Waldgirmes also confirms the manufacture of tools on site.

Two pottery kilns, one of which was located in an artisan's house, provide evidence for the potter's trade. Although no misfirings from the production are found, the work pits of the kilns contained layers of ashes that indicate successful firing processes. Another pottery kiln in a different part of the settlement remained unfinished.

Scythe and sickle fragments point to agricultural activity. The extent to which this was a specialised occupation cannot be determined from the present findings. Gardening as a sideline or for self-sufficiency would have been possible within the settlement as well as in its surroundings.

The processing of non-ferrous metal was practised in Waldgirmes to some extent, as clearly shown by finds of casting waste and crucible fragments. The tool inventory of this craft is still to be investigated in connection with the selected finds. RS

Slag as evidence of iron processing.

PRECISE HISTORIC DATA

Historical facts about the founding of the Roman settlement in Waldgirmes are provided by an analysis of the coins discovered during the excavations as well as by the pottery, especially the Terra Sigillata. Even more precise data can be obtained from dendrochronological studies of the preserved wood. The earliest timbers from the wells of the settlement were felled between the fall or winter of 4 BC and the spring of 3 BC. Therefore, the first buildings in the settlement will have been erected no later than 3 BC. The town's Forum, however, was built on top of an older, unfinished complex, which will have been begun even earlier.

To determine the time of the Roman withdrawal, the ladders found in the wells can offer valuable information: the trees from which they were made were cut down between the fall of AD 9 and the spring of AD 10.

The destruction of the statues on the Forum and their deposition in the well most likely took place after Varus' catastrophic defeat at the hands of Germanic tribes in AD 9. The filling-in of Well 2, in which the ladders and the horse's head were found, can therefore only have occurred later than AD 9.

Nevertheless, even after this major event, Waldgirmes still played an essential role as a military base during Germanicus' campaigns against the Chatti. This is evidenced by improvements made to the main street, probably in AD 15. With the cessation of military operations on the orders of Emperor Tiberius in AD 16, the story of Waldgirmes also comes to an end.

This precise dating of the founding of Waldgirmes has fundamentally changed the picture of Roman rule in Germania at the time of the first Roman emperor, Augustus. The results of the archaeological excavations suggest that Publius Quinctilius Varus did indeed administer a Roman province on the right bank of the Rhine, serving as its governor. The middle Lahn valley was the hub of the marching routes of Roman soldiers during their campaigns of conquest in Germania. The choice of this site for the establishment of the new settlement, therefore, seems logical and quite understandable from a strategic point of view.   CA

VARUS' COUNTERMARK

Coin of Augustus
from Well 2.
Bronze, so-called
"Lugdunum type" with
countermark of Varus.
Also see photo on p. 27.

With the Roman campaigns of conquest, large quantities of silver and bronze coins from various mints of the Roman Empire were brought to the newly conquered lands.

During the excavations in Waldgirmes, a total of 337 Roman coins were unearthed, of which 228 were sufficiently well-preserved to be identified. Among these, none had been struck after AD 9, the year of the Varian defeat. Fourteen coins from a series minted at Lugdunum (Lyon) in Gaul bear an additional countermark - that of Publius Quinctilius Varus. Countermarks were often used to denote special payments to the legions. Such monetary gifts were usually given to the soldiers on the occasion of an imperial visit, or to reward a military success. Varus began his governorship in Germania in AD 7. So these coins must date to the years AD 7–9.

One of these precisely dated, countermarked coins from the Lugdunum series is of particular importance because it was discovered in Well 2, where the bronze horse head was found. This coin lay on the edge of the barrel that formed the lowest part of the well shaft and was exceptionally well preserved.

In addition to the Roman coinage, a wide range of Celtic coins was also found; apparently, they were still among the coins in circulation in the early Roman settlement.   CA

FINE TABLEWARE FROM FRANCE AND ITALY

Only a small fraction of the ceramics found in Waldgirmes belong to the upmarket type of Roman tableware known as "Terra Sigillata". Characteristic of such wares are the fine clay and the glossy reddish glaze. Beginning in the early 1st century BC, manufactories produced these vessels in large quantities, usually stamping their pottery with a manufacturers mark. Terra Sigillata was widely sold from Italy throughout the entire Roman Empire. Throughout the 1st century BC, additional production centres were set up in southern and central Gaul.

During the excavations, many – in-part tiny and poorly preserved – sherds from Terra Sigillata vessels came to light. Roughly 250 fragments could be attributed to specific ceramic forms. Among these were 8 platters, 110 plates and 140 bowls. Only a few vessels could be reconstructed entirely.

Aided by chemical analyses, we can pinpoint the place of origin for many ceramics. Pottery reached Waldgirmes from Lyon and Champagne in Gaul, as well as from Pisa and Arezzo in Italy.   CA

EVERYDAY DISHES

Potsherds are the most common finds in any settlement. Only rarely can complete vessels be reassembled from the mass of fragments. Roman vessels were thrown on the quickly rotating potter's wheel; in contrast, Germanic pots were built up by hand, so they tended to be thick-walled and coarser. Therefore, it is usually easy to distinguish between Roman and Germanic potsherds.

The majority of the ceramic finds are wheel-thrown Roman pottery for everyday use. The fine Belgian Ware was, like Terra Sigillata, most often imported. However, the discovery of two pottery kilns shows that ceramics were also made locally. Among the potsherds, the red (Terra Rubra) and the black-to-grey Belgian Ware (Terra Nigra) can be clearly distinguished. Some of the vessels bear a potters stamp. Ornamental borders, created with small wheels, often decorate the larger vessels. Among the most common forms of Belgian Ware are plates and beakers.

Pitchers, grating bowls and cookware for everyday use were made of rough, hardwearing pottery.   CA

AMPHORAE — OIL AND CONDIMENTS FROM SPAIN

The most important transport container in Roman times was the two-handled amphora made of fired clay. In Waldgirmes a large number of amphora fragments were found; they came from the different types of amphorae in which a wide variety of Mediterranean products were conveyed to the Lahn valley.

The majority of these sherds belonged to oil amphorae, followed by vessels for wine, olives and condiments such as fish sauce (garum). Two-thirds of the amphorae were made on the Iberian Peninsula, while the rest came from Italy, the eastern Mediterranean and the Rhône valley in Gaul.

The data shows that all the oil and olives delivered to Waldgirmes came from the province of Hispania, more specifically the valley of the Guadalquivir River in southern Spain. The popular condiments were almost exclusively products from that area. The wine, however, came mostly from Italy and the eastern part of the Roman Empire.

Pitcher for serving wine, oil or water

This outline of the production places of the transport containers and the goods shipped convincingly proves the close connection between the Mediterranean region and the Lahn Valley in the far northwest of the Imperium. **CA**

Foot of an amphora

HANDMADE LOCAL POTTERY

The locally produced ceramics in Waldgirmes consist primarily of handmade wares, which were occasionally finished on a slowly turning potter's wheel. The potsherds are very small so that no complete vessels could be reassembled. The most common forms are simple barrel-shaped pots and flat plates – types also used in pre-Roman times. These ceramics mainly served as cookware. But vessels of simple, regular shape with the largest diameter in the upper third, different tureen forms and large storage vessels can also be identified from the sherds.

Approximately 15% of all the handmade potsherds display decorations, created with various techniques. Most commonly, fingertip impressions are seen in the rim zone of the vessel. Many sherds are daubed with clay slip. Fine or rough, irregular and bow-shaped lines were applied with a potter's comb. Other types of decoration use fingernail and imprints of cereal grains. Incised decorations occur in hanging-triangle and closed fir-tree patterns.

Connections to the nearby settlement (oppidum) on the Dünsberg, which was populated up to the second half of the 1st century BC (the late La-Tène period), are particularly apparent in the local pottery. This could mean that at least some groups of people, after abandoning the fortified hilltop settlement, remained in the Lahn valley. **CA**

BRONZE CASTING AND METALWORK

In addition to the statue fragments, a few small finds made of bronze also came to light in Wald-girmes, such as writing utensils, mirror and vessel fragments, bells, brooches and bronze rings. Such jewellery and everyday objects were made, processed and repaired in the settlement. A workshop used for metalworking could be identified in the northeastern part of town where the spacious shed-like buildings stood. Fragments of foundry crucibles, as well as casting waste in the form of slag and sprues, are the remnants of bronze casting. During subsequent processing, punches and burins were used for piercing as well as engraving, while chasing tools were used for marking and ornamenting. Files, grinding- and polishing stones were used for shaping and treating the surfaces. All of these tools appear in the find inventory. Among the most notable metalworking tools are the articulated shears, used to cut sheet metal, and a mushroom-shaped anvil with a domed face, used for beating metal.

Of the tools discussed here, not all are exclusively used in processing non-ferrous metal; some can also be employed to work pieces made of iron or precious metal.

RS

AN UNUSUAL DEPOT

In Well 2 there were eight intact millstones made of basalt; they came from handmills and were between 35-40 cm in diameter. They appear to have been deposited together with the horse head. None of the three upper stones (rubbing stones) or the five lower stones (bedstones) can be combined to form a complete grinding mechanism. All the metal parts of the hand-mills were missing: presumably, they had been removed for reuse.

Such a find is unique up until now, especially since the stones were all in a usable condition when placed in the well. Seven stones show various degrees of wear and tear, while one is a nearly finished product. Chemical analysis shows that the raw material for the millstones came from the ancient quarries of the Eifel near Mayen. The blanks were evidently delivered to Waldgirmes, where the final processing took place.

Besides the intact millstones, there were some additional millstone fragments in the well that – in comparison to the intact stones – were completely worn down. The disposal of such useless pieces in pits or wells was quite common.

At other findspots in Waldgirmes, fragments of five large millstones made of sandstone were found. With diameters of around 50 cm and weights of 50 kg per stone, they will have belonged to stationary mills in the area of the settlement. The precise locations of these mills could not be determined from the excavated evidence.   RS

THE COMMON WEAPONRY

For a Roman settlement beyond the borders of the Roman Empire, the protection afforded by the presence of soldiers was an absolute necessity. In Waldgirmes, building footprints can be identified that correspond to the usual troop barracks from Roman military camps; a demarcated military area, however, cannot be proved.

In the settlement with its predominantly civilian character, only a limited number of pieces of military equipment are among the finds. These are mostly fragments of the common weapons of the period such as pilum points: one of which, with its partially preserved shaft, has a total length of 16.5 cm. The typical leaf-shaped spear point is also in evidence, with its rhombic cross-section and perforated socket for attachment to the wooden shaft. Some of the pieces could be projectile points, but due to their state of preservation, this cannot be proven. In some cases, they may also be fittings from the end of throwing- or thrusting weapons – the so-called "lance-shoes". From a Roman dagger (pugio), a fragment of the handle and possibly the tip of the blade, which has a cutting edge on both sides, survive. A diamond-shaped shield fitting and a probable shield nail represent the defensive weapons. Among the unmistakable items of military equipment are also fragments of two helmet crest mounts.

In addition to other finds, such as a bronze strap clamp and two iron tent nails, comparable pieces from different military contexts are known. However, it is also possible that these items were used in the civilian realm.

Except for two fully preserved spear points, all the militaria survive only in fragments. It can be assumed that these were intended for recycling or – in the case of the smaller pieces – were merely lost. RS

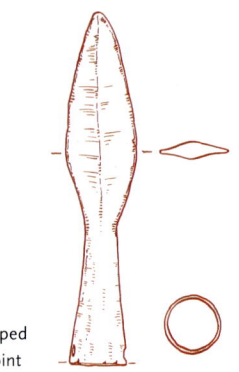

Leaf-shaped
spear point

WOOD AND IRON

Woodworking equipment is represented by a number of very different tools. The delimbing knife is commonly used for cutting rods and the bark peeler for removing bark from logs, thus both are evidence for activities related to raw material extraction. The chisels were put to use for cutting wood joints, the small carving knife for the finer shaping of wood, while the splitting knife was probably employed in the production of shingles. Based on the finds, only individual tasks within the woodworking trade can be documented; other tools essential for logging, carpentry and cabinetmaking, such as axes, saws, rasps and planes, are completely missing.

The blacksmithing trade, too, can only be incompletely recognised in the tool inventory. The lancet-shaped fire shovel with a twisted handle, whose shape is unusual for Roman sites, will presumably be associated with this craft. By contrast, tools for cutting iron (chisels and hammers) are entirely missing from the finds. The products of blacksmithing, on the other hand, are available in a variety of forms, many of which were undoubtedly made by local artisans.   RS

Mushroom-shaped anvil

Lancet-shaped fire shovel

STONE, LEATHER AND LEAD

Evidence of stoneworking is found in Waldgirmes to some extent. The few stone building foundations were constructed using locally available limestone ("Lahnmarmor"), wet-joined with lime mortar. Some basalt fragments of a small basin, as well as presumed stepping-stones for pedestrians, also come from local sources and may have been processed locally. The pedestals for the statues on the Forum, on the other hand, consisted of imported shell limestone from the Metz region. This soft material could be efficiently worked with common tools such as chisels, knives, and scrapers, which are often also associated with other crafts.

Leatherworking is also revealed in archaeological evidence from the settlement. Especially notable are several scrapers or scraping knives, used for smoothing skins. In the case of other tools, similar to the scrapers mentioned, it is unclear whether they were used for leatherworking, in making pottery or in the medical realm.

Lead was used for making water pipes, among other things, as evidenced by fragments of lead pipes and traces of lead casting in the roadside ditches. This soft, supple metal was also well suited to making repairs. The lead clamp used to patch-up a Dolium (a large earthenware vessel) is clear evidence of this practice (see photo, above).   RS

DOMESTIC TASKS AND HOUSEHOLD GOODS

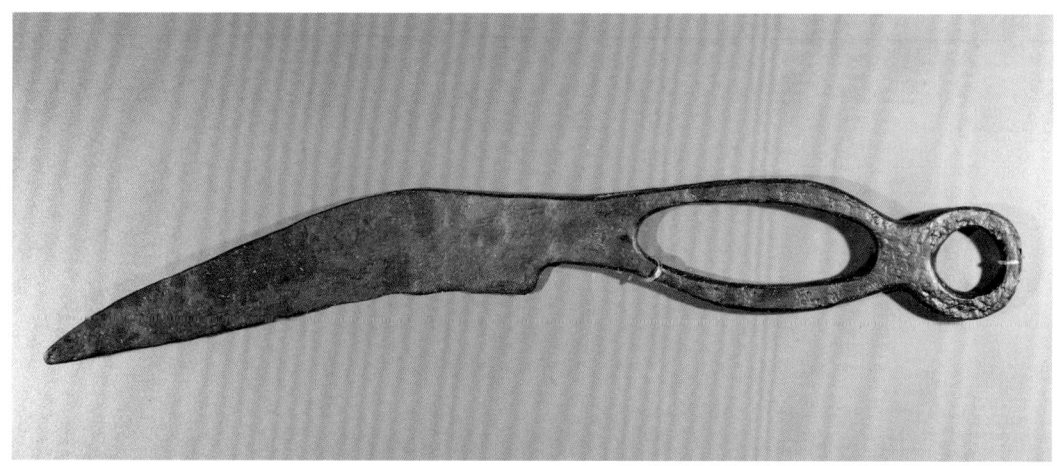

two broken bow-shears, a bodkin and a sewing needle with eyelet are just as much a part of the textile craft as are the spindle whorls of various designs.

Objects from the everyday life of Waldgirmes' inhabitants cover the entire spectrum expected in such a settlement. In addition to pottery of varying quality, there are additional household items, such as box fittings, keys, chains and parts of scales. Even personal items such as jewellery, writing utensils, and shoe nails are represented in the find material.   RS

In many cases, tools and equipment were not necessarily associated with specific trades, but instead were used in the domestic sphere. Among other items, these include the 16 identifiable knives of differing shapes and sizes. Knives were present as universal tools in all households and of course were brought along when needed outside the home. Accordingly, they occasionally have a ring pommel at the end of the handle for suspension or attachment to the belt. The elegantly shaped, small knife with pierced handle shown here displays a good example of this.

Textile processing is an activity that to a considerable extent should be regarded as a domestic task. The

INTAGLIO

This multi-coloured intaglio made of glass paste was found (without its original setting) in a roadside ditch. The glass paste, from which the gemstone was made, deserves special attention. The blanks were made in moulds. First, two strips of opaque white glass were placed in the mould and secured with a layer of light blue glass. Then a thin layer of yellow glass was applied to the upper and lower third of the intaglio, while a layer of white glass was added in the central section. The final layer was light blue. Through this mixture of different tones, the desired colour scheme with green and dark blue sections and opaque white banding was created. These glass paste gems resembled agates but achieved shades that did not occur in nature.

The image shows a standing, left-facing Niobid, who clasps one of her murdered brothers in her arms. According to the legend, the Goddess Leto – motivated by jealousy – commanded her children Apollon and Artemis to kill all the children of Niobe. Only two children survived, including Chloris, who is depicted in this scene. EL

RING WITH INTAGLIO

The iron finger ring with a carnelian intaglio comes from the fill material of Well 2 – in which the horse head also lay – and was extracted with a soil sample from the lower part of the roughly 10 m deep well. It lay in the upper part of the wooden barrel that made up the lowest section of the well's lining.

The iron ring was severely corroded and is also bent. The good-quality intaglio bears a portrait of Dionysius. The God of Wine wears a wreath of grape leaves on his head; he stands relaxedly, his weight on his right foot, and glances over his right shoulder at the end of a Thrysus, which lies casually across his shoulders.

EL

SILVER PENDANT

The tiny silver pendant lay in a pit at the back of a larger complex of buildings in the southeastern part of the settlement. The building's broad portico opened onto the main east-west street. The structure's location and layout suggest that it was a shop.

The pendant, only 18mm long, is rhomboid-shaped. The loop is moulded and decorated with notches. A horizontal rib divides the loop from the body. The edges of the rhomboid body are set off by fine grooves.

The shape of the pendant resembles the Egyptian symbol for life (the Ankh). As with the mosaic bead, an Egyptian pictorial motif has been adopted here, a custom that was common well into the 1st century.

EL

Original size

Original size

MOSAIC GLASS BEAD

Among the approximately 20 beads unearthed during the excavations, some of very high quality, this mosaic glass bead particularly stands out.

For the production of mosaic glass, differently coloured glass rods are first melted together to form a single rod, creating the desired image. From this, thin slices are cut off and fused with the rest of the bead.

Around the small bead, which is only 15 mm in diameter, three identical images are repeated. They portray the black and white bull, Apis, the embodiment of the Egyptian god, Ptah. Between his horns, he bears the sun. Before him stands a small altar on which a burnt offering is made. A thin yellow line marks the ground below the animal, while the scene is enclosed in a yellow frame.

Between the three pictorial motifs lie fields of light green glass; the rest of the bead is made of opaque, light blue glass. The mosaic bead was pierced perpendicular to the image so that it could be worn as a pendant.

EL

EYE FIBULA

The almost entirely intact silver brooch is of Germanic origin and is classified as an eye fibula because of the pierced "eyes" in the head plate.

Two rows of punching decorate the bow of the fibula. The fibula foot has indented lines on its upper and lower faces that create a geometric design. Originally, two decorative knobs were attached to the head plate, but only one survived.

A total of 42 fibulae are known from the Waldgirmes site, among which are two additional eye fibulae made of bronze; they, however, are more poorly preserved. The silver eye fibula came from one of the roadside ditches: its wearer will undoubtedly have lost it.

The eye fibulae have their main areas of distribution in Central Germany, the Bohemian Basin and the middle Rhine. Their appearance at Roman military sites in the Rhineland is associated with the presence of auxiliary troops of Germanic origin in Roman military camps. EL

Original size

SILVER DISC FIBULA

The intricately wrought silver fibula has a round base plate encircled by a beaded rim. A blossom made of pierced sheet silver is held in place by a central rivet. Around a red glass inlay that covers the rivet, there spreads a garland of eight lotus leaves, each in turn set with dark blue glass inlays. The wreath of leaves and the beaded rim were gilded, while the inner circle of petals shone silver against the lotus leaves.

A loop-hinge pin served to hold the jewelled disc in position; it was riveted to the underside of the base plate.

Based on stylistic considerations – such as proximity to the Etruscans design idiom – the origin of this piece of jewellery is thought to be Upper or Central Italy. The disc fibula was discovered intact, with its pin closed, in a roadside ditch. Perhaps it had not been lost, but rather – as is known from the Gallic and Germanic cultures – deliberately deposited.   EL

Original size

MILLEFIORI-GLASS

Among the few glass finds from Waldgirmes, this small fragment of a mosaic glass bowl stands out. Mosaic glassware is made from a number of differently coloured pieces of glass.

A wide variety of glass elements may be used, including simple colours, stripes or more elaborate patterns cut from fused, multi-coloured glass rods. Depending on the fineness and the size of the individual mosaic elements, the quality of the finished vessel can vary greatly. The small sherd from Waldgirmes, with its large-scale elements, certainly does not count among the best-crafted pieces, especially since the grinding of its inner side was quite poorly done.

The individual glass pieces are fused together to create a circular sheet of glass, whose rim is often folded over a rod as a termination. The soft, hot glass sheet is then lowered into a mould whose interior corresponds to the desired shape of the vessel.

After it hardens, the vessel is removed from the mould, finished by grinding inside and out, and then polished. EL

TIMELINE

SIGNIFICANT EVENTS

58–51 BC Caesar conquers Gaul.
The Rhine becomes the border of the Germanic settlement areas.

44 BC Caesar is murdered.

12–9 BC Drusus campaigns in Germania; he advances as far as the River Elbe.

7/5 BC Construction of Roman military base at Haltern.

4 BC–AD 16 Foundation and existence of the Roman settlement at Waldgirmes in the valley of the River Lahn near Giessen.

AD 4–6 Successful expedition by Tiberius into Germania east of the Rhine.

AD 9 Roman forces under General Varus are defeated by Germanic troops led by Arminius.

AD 13–16 Germanicus, son of Drusus, is Commander-in-Chief of the Rhineland troops.

AD 15/16 Revenge campaigns of Germanicus against the Germans east of the Rhine.

AD 16 Germanicus is recalled. The Rhine River again becomes the border of the Empire.

AD 39 Expedition of Gaius Caligula into Germania.

AD 73/74 Conquest and consolidation of territory east of the Rhine by Cn. Pinarius Clemens. Construction of direct road connections from the Rhine to the Danube.

AD 81–85 Emperor Domitian wages war against the Germanic Chatti.

AD 85 The two Roman military districts on the Rhine become the provinces Germania Inferior (capital Cologne) and Germania Superior (capital Mainz).

AD 88/89 Unsuccessful revolt led by Governor of Upper Germany, L. Antonius Saturninus, accompanied by considerable destruction in the Rhine-Main area.

Early 2nd c. AD The Upper German-Raetian Limes is laid out as a patrol path with timber watchtowers. A Numerus is stationed at the Saalburg Pass.

REIGNS OF ROMAN EMPERORS

27 BC–AD 14 Augustus

AD 14–37 Tiberius

AD 37–41 Caligula

AD 41–54 Claudius

AD 54–68 Nero

AD 68/69 "Year of the Four Emperors" – Galba, Otho, Vitellius, Vespasian

AD 69–79 Vespasian

AD 79–81 Titus

AD 81–96 Domitian

AD 96–98 Nerva

AD 98–117 Trajan

BIBLIOGRAPHY

A. Becker/G. Rasbach, Waldgirmes – Die Ausgrabungen in der spätaugusteischen Siedlung von Lahnau-Waldgirmes (1993–2009). 1. Befunde und Funde. Römisch-Germanische Forschungen Bd. 71 (Darmstadt 2015).

A. Becker/G. Rasbach/H.-J. Köhler, Der römische Stützpunkt von Waldgirmes. Archäologische Denkmäler in Hessen 148 (Wiesbaden 1999).

P. C. Bol, Antike Bronzetechnik. Kunst und Handwerk antiker Erzbildner (München 1985).

K. Bringmann, Augustus. Gestalten der Antike (Darmstadt 2007).

G. Lahusen/E. Formigli, Römische Bildnisse aus Bronze. Kunst und Technik (München 2001).

Landesverband Lippe/Museum und Park Kalkriese/ LWL Römermuseum Haltern am See (Hg.), 2000 Jahre Varusschlacht. Imperium – Konflikt – Mythos. 3 Bände (Stuttgart 2009).

Landschaftsverband Rheinland (Hg.), Krieg und Frieden. Kelten – Römer – Germanen (Bonn und Darmstadt 2007).

D. Rohde/H. Schneider (Hg.), Hessen in der Antike. Die Chatten vom Zeitalter der Römer bis zur Alltagskultur der Gegenwart (Kassel 2006).

C. Rolley, Die griechischen Bronzen (München 1984).

Staatliche Museen Preußischer Kulturbesitz (Hg.), Kaiser Augustus und die verlorene Republik (Berlin 1988).

P. Cornelius Tacitus, Germania. Herausgegeben u. kommentiert v. A. Lund (Heidelberg 1988).

G. Uelsberg u.a. (Hg.), Gebrochener Glanz. Römische Großbronzen am Unesco-Welterbe Limes (Mainz 2014).

L. Wamser, Die Römer zwischen Alpen und Nordmeer. Zivilisatorisches Erbe einer europäischen Militärmacht (Mainz 2000).

IMPRESSUM

48 pages with 48 illustrations

Carsten Amrhein, Elke Löhnig and Rüdiger Schwarz, Rome in Germania. Waldgirmes – Permanent Exhibition in the Saalburg Roman Fort (Oppenheim am Rhein 2019)

Bibliographic information published by the Deutsche Nationalbibliothek

The German National Library lists this publication in the Deutschen Nationalbibliografie; detailed bibliographic data are available on the Internet at http://dnb.d-nb.de

© 2019 by Nünnerich-Asmus Verlag & Media, Oppenheim am Rhein and Römerkastell Saalburg, Bad Homburg v.d.H.

ISBN 978-3-96176-099-2

Design: Elisabeth Pangels, komplus GmbH, Heidelberg

Editors: Elke Löhnig, Römerkastell Saalburg, Luca Barba, Nünnerich-Asmus Verlag & Media.

English translation: Carola Murray-Seegert, Oberursel

Printed by:
Grafisches Centrum Cuno GmbH & CO. KG. Calbe

Sources of Illustrations
Becker/Rasbach, Waldgirmes Fig. 76 (O. Braasch, 29.5.1999): 18;
Becker/Rasbach, Waldgirmes Figs. 57/58 (hessenARCHÄOLOGIE, U. Schreiber): 20; Fig. 128: 36; Fig. 175: 41 r.; Fig 117: 43 below; Fig. 125: 44 r.;
Faber-Courtial, Darmstadt: 23;
hessenARCHÄOLOGIE, P. Odvody: 3, 8–11, 47, outside front cover l., outside back cover l.;
Ranger Design Stuttgart, P. Fajt: 28, outside front cover r., outside back cover r.;
Rolley, Griech. Bronzen (pattern): 7;
Römerkastell Saalburg, Elke Löhnig: 1, 6, 12–14, 25, 27, 29–34, 37, 39–45;
Römerkastell Saalburg, Marion Nickel: 16;
Römisch-Germanische Kommission, G. Rasbach: 15;
Römisch-Germanische Kommission: 4–5, 35, inside back cover.